M Y   T H E O L O G Y

AF272985

FINDING GOD
IN THE UNIVERSE

MY THEOLOGY

GUY CONSOLMAGNO

FINDING GOD IN THE UNIVERSE

DARTON · LONGMAN + TODD

First published in 2021 by
Darton, Longman and Todd Ltd
1 Spencer Court
140 – 142 Wandsworth High Street
London SW18 4JJ

ISBN: 978-1-913657-54-3

A catalogue record for this book is available from the
British Library.

Printed and bound in Great Britain by
Bell & Bain, Glasgow

Contents

1

Learning to Look

A fundamental truth about finding God
in the universe is that if you already know
God is present, then you can see God
everywhere; but if you don't expect to
find God, then you don't even think
to look, and so God goes unseen.
In order to find God, you have to
have the faith to be able to
look for God.

Do you know what day it is today?

I've reached the age where I need to take daily pills for cholesterol and blood pressure and the like. They are stored in a set of convenient little plastic boxes, each one labeled with the day of the week. Sometimes, first thing in the morning, reading the day of the week from my pill dispenser is the only way I know that today is Thursday.

The day of the week is something that I am expected to remember, even if it takes a little effort at first ... if for no other reason than to keep my various appointments in order, and to know where to look on my calendar to keep me in tune with my schedule for the day.

Back when I did a lot of travel, I often would wake up in a strange city not remembering where I was or even what continent I was on. Usually it wouldn't take more than a minute looking around the bedroom to remind me. But that moment to orient myself was essential before I could even figure out which side of the bed to roll out of and not bump into a wall.

If you're nodding in recognition, I need say no more. On the other hand, if you're smirking at my old-man cluelessness, let me challenge you in a different way. Do you know what the phase of the Moon is right now?

The phases of the Moon are connected with the heights of the tides, of course, so sailors and fishermen and other folks living near the sea might be interested. Traditionally, hunters and harvesters planned their activities in the fall around the nights near full Moon. Stargazers, both amateur and professional, need to know where the Moon is if they want to observe it, or if they want to avoid trying to observe faint stars near a Moon that is particularly bright. But if you don't fit any of those categories, you probably have no reason to pay much attention to the Moon.

You can often find the different phases of the Moon indicated right there on the same calendar that tells you it's Thursday and you have a dentist appointment at three. But you don't need a calendar to know which phase the Moon is. Assuming your vision is in relatively good shape, and the skies are not cloudy all day, you can just go look for yourself. The Moon is the one astronomical object (besides the Sun) that you can see nearly any day or night, at some time during the day, even in the face of our modern rampant city light pollution.

Yet how many of us even bother to look?

I teach an astronomy class to high school students, and one of the tasks I set them every term is to try to find the Moon at least once a week and then report back what it looked like ... its phase and its position in the sky. My hope is that they will learn to recognize the patterns in the Moon's changing shape and location. It's surprisingly difficult for many of them. Certainly the Moon can't be that hard to see? But who's in the habit of looking for it?

Will they see how the phases of the Moon progress from crescent to half to full, then back down to crescent but with the curve of the crescent facing the opposite way? Will they notice that the crescent Moons can be seen in the dark only just after sunset, or just before sunrise, near the horizon? Will they notice that, during the evening hours, the crescent Moon is always in the west, the full Moon always in the east? Will they discover that sometimes you can actually see the Moon during daytime hours?

Even assuming clear skies, there will be many evenings in a month when the Moon is not visible. Do they notice that these moonless evenings occur together, for maybe ten days in a row or so, every month? Will they be able to notice that the moonless evenings occur when the Moon is waning?

Do they notice that the Moon's rhythms are not really monthly, but recur over a period slightly longer than four weeks, but slightly shorter than a full calendar month?

I have yet to find a high school student who has been able work out all of these different patterns for themselves. Too often they just report what they expect to see, not what they've actually observed. Or they try making it up, which is ridiculously easy to spot. (You never see a crescent Moon at midnight; nor do you ever find the Moon in the northern sky – at least, not from the northern hemisphere.)

But mostly it's hard for them – as for most of us – to leave their comfortable rooms to go outside and look up in the sky at night ... or even to think of looking at the Moon when they're already outdoors during the evening, on their way home from a concert or out to get a pizza. It's hard to remember to look. It's even harder to pay attention to what you see, much less to recognize that what you can see tonight is different from last night but not all that different from a month ago.

The analogy to prayer jumps out at me.

Like God, the Moon is always there, even if we can't see it. It's not always easy to find. Sometimes it has set and won't rise again for another ten or twelve hours. Sometimes it's obscured by clouds. But even when we can't see it, even when it is on the other side of the world from us, it's still there.

And of course, there are those of us who cannot see the Moon because of a physical disability, like loss of sight. But even they can feel the sunlight during the day, the cool breath of the wind at night. They can hear the sounds of nature as dogs howl at the Full Moon or hide in the darkness of the New Moon. And if nothing else, they know about the Moon from those of us who have seen it. I know professional astronomers who are physically blind but still actively contribute to the field; they see the universe in their minds' eyes.

But, like God, even when the Moon is brilliant and full in a clear dark sky and your eyes are clear and sharp, you still may not notice it if you don't bother to look.

Of course, like all analogies, this one fails if you push it too far. The activity of looking at the Moon is completely one-sided. The Moon is a lifeless hunk of rock; it doesn't care if I look for it. God, on the other hand, offers love to us before waiting for our response, and can make Himself more or less visible depending on how we respond. That's a two-way street.

And the position of the Moon on any night, at any moment, can be calculated. You can know ahead of time where the Moon will be, put it on your calendar, and plan accordingly. But there is no calculus to tell you when God will be trying to get your attention.

That makes it all the more surprising, therefore, that both looking for the Moon and looking for God can provide a common feedback. Doing that looking satisfies a common urge. What is that urge? Why do we look?

A dog or a cat has no need to know where the Moon is. If they are fed and petted, their lives are satisfied. Yet even a dog may bay at the Moon. For us human beings, though, baying is not enough. There is a deeper hunger we have which both astronomy and religion speak to ... a hunger that goes beyond bread alone. What is that hunger that I satisfy by looking at the Moon?

Meanwhile, looking at the Moon is only the beginning. Once you start looking up at the sky at night, the tiny, brilliant stars dotting the dome overhead can evoke awe and wonder. I wonder, can dogs and cats even see them? Some migrating birds do, I am told. But even migrating birds don't react with the questions we have: What are the stars? Why are they there? Why do we live in a universe with stars? And why do we find them so beautiful?

Alas, for most people, the stars are much harder to see nowadays than they used to be, thanks to all the useless city light that pollutes our nighttime sky. Pope Benedict in an Easter vigil homily once compared light pollution to human sinfulness: blotting out God's lights with our own artificial light. As a result, the view of a truly dark sky is rare, and for someone not used to seeing what the sky ought to look like it can inspire both awe and fear. Again, it's not unlike the way we react to suddenly being aware of God's presence.

When I was a child I spent my summers at a cottage by Lake Huron in the 'thumb' of Michigan, distant from city lights, and the nighttime sky was full of the Moon and the stars. I learned the names of the brighter stars from my father, who had loved to look at the stars himself when he was a boy. He had also been trained in celestial navigation while flying for the American Army Air Corps during World War II. To him, the stars were both a source of joy and an essential aspect of a most deadly business.

When I was around ten years old I was given a copy of the famous book by H. A. Rey, *The Stars: A New Way to See Them*, which taught me not only the bright stars but the fainter constellations as well. H. A. Rey was the fellow who wrote and drew the *Curious George* children's stories; his skill as both artist and writer brought the constellations to life. (And he and his wife were Jewish refugees from Nazi Germany during my father's war.)

Unlike many other astronomy books I'd used before, Rey referred to the constellations by their English names, making it easier for a kid like me to recognize them and remember them. Their names became keys to stories I could hear in my own language, about queens and princes and sea monsters, lions and dragons and bears. In that way, the constellations became a way of getting in touch with the ancients who had named them.

'"Arcturus" is his other name— *I'd rather call him "Star"',* wrote the poet Emily Dickinson. *'It's very mean of Science to go and interfere!'* I was furious when I read that. I wanted to know my friends' names. I would never call a friend, 'boy', or a beloved pet, 'dog'.

I wanted to be able to go outside and, like a character that H. A. Rey drew in his book, gesture to the sky and say, 'Look! There's Arcturus!' I wanted to know how to star-hop ... to trace a curve from the handle of the Big Dipper to a distinctive orange star and then down to a brilliant white one: to 'arc to Arcturus and spike to Spica'. I wanted to be able to recognize my favorite stars not only by their location, but by their colors and brightnesses. I wanted to know their histories, where they live in our galaxy (are they near or far?), and what they were up to in their stellar evolution.

When I enrolled at MIT (mostly as an excuse to hang out at its science fiction library) I chose to study the closest thing to astronomy that I could find in the catalogue — planetary sciences — in no small part because of my love of looking at the stars and knowing them by name. And in those science fiction stories, planets were places where people had adventures. I wanted to know more about places that up to now had been nothing more than settings for adventures, or dots of light with ancient names.

After MIT I moved on to graduate studies in planetary sciences at the University of Arizona. My first week there, I went up to a university telescope in the Catalina Mountains north of Tucson with some fellow graduate students and I was awed by the clear desert view. Then one of my fellow students struck a familiar pose and said, 'Look! There's Arcturus!' I could only laugh. We'd both read that H. A. Rey book! I knew I was where I belonged.

Eight years later, I wasn't so sure. By then I had finished my doctoral degree and spent too many years spinning my wheels in temporary research positions. Astronomy had become just a job. I rarely went outdoors to look at the stars anymore. Instead, in the wee hours of the morning I would lie awake in bed, stare at my apartment ceiling, and wonder, 'Why am I worrying about computer models for the moons of Saturn when there are people starving in the world?'

So I quit. And to salve my conscience a little, I decided to join the US Peace Corps ... maybe do something about starving people. My sister had been in the Peace Corps, so I knew something about it from her. But the idea of leaving my home, my books, my friends for two years and living in a third-world country was so absolutely crazy, so completely unlike me, that even today I can't really understand what drove me to such an extreme action.

And of course, once I found myself in Peace Corps training, learning Swahili in a remote part of Kenya, the enormity of my stupidity had become obvious. I was so uncomfortable, so out of place, so disoriented that I became physically ill. While the rest of our training group went off on field trips, the trainers kept me behind at the training camp. My own discomfort had become so acute that I wasn't fit to travel.

One night, alone in the training camp, I came to the obvious conclusion. I was not where I belonged, and it was madness to think that I could endure. The Peace Corps had made it clear to all of us that if anyone ever wanted to go home, they'd send you back on the next plane, no questions asked. It was time to take that option.

Except ... I had brought my copy of the H. A. Rey book with me, and it had star charts for observing all around the world, including stars visible when you were somewhere like Kenya, on the equator. I had always wanted to see the Southern Cross. Was I far enough south? Would it be up any time this night? I should certainly take advantage of my time on the equator to see it if I could; I couldn't imagine I would ever travel so far from home again.

The book did not fail me. It told me that the Southern Cross would rise above the horizon at about 4 a.m.. So finally, at peace with my decision, I went to bed and told myself to wake up at four.

Thus it was that in the early morning hours I got out of bed and went outdoors for one last look under African skies. In the southeast, in a sky far from city lights and more full of stars than I had ever seen before, there was The Southern Cross in all its glory: a bright little kite-shaped diamond of stars. My last reason for staying in Kenya had been fulfilled. I could go home.

Turning to walk back to the dorm where I was staying, I was not prepared for what I saw next. There on the northern horizon was the familiar shape of the Big Dipper. Following the stars of its handle I could 'arc to Arcturus' — yes!

The glorious constellations of winter, Orion and Gemini and Taurus, were setting to the west. The summer triangle of stars, Vega and Deneb and Altair, the stars my father had taught me, were rising in the east. Overhead, strutting in all its glory like it had just leapt up there from a nearby game park, was the glorious constellation of Leo the Lion.

I knew them all. They were my friends, the stars I had called by name since childhood.

And at that moment, I was oriented. I knew where I was, even if I didn't quite know why I was there just yet. I was no longer homesick; I was home. Wherever I could see the stars of my childhood I would never be away from home.

And so, to leave this place would be absolute madness.

I spent the next two years in Kenya, learning to live in a culture and a language that I would never have expected to love so dearly. I was an outsider, of course; but then, I had always felt like an outsider even in America, at least now in Kenya it made sense to feel that way. And whenever things got to feel just a little too foreign, I could look up at the stars and reorient myself.

(Since then I've traveled from Iceland to Antarctica and several times around the world. I always keep an eye out for the night sky to look for familiar constellations ... including now the centaurs and peacocks and wolves of the southern hemisphere.)

Seeing that I had a doctorate in an astronomical science, the Peace Corps sent me to teach physics at the University of Nairobi, and there I discovered how much I loved to teach. Meanwhile, every weekend I wound up traveling by myself on local buses and jitney cabs, *matatus*, to places I had never been before, with no one I knew for miles around, en route up country to the schools where my Peace Corps friends taught ... staying in mud huts under mosquito netting, giving talks to the local folks and showing them the Moon and planets in my little telescope.

Ah, my little telescope. I had had a small telescope when I was a kid, and I knew how to use it to see craters on the Moon, or the little moons orbiting Jupiter, or even the rings of Saturn. When I went off to Kenya, my friend Dan helped me choose a telescope to take with me: a compact but powerful bit of optics which also doubled as a telephoto lens, perfect for the game parks. And when I set it up at my friends' schools I discovered that the people in Kenya were hungry to see the rings of Saturn, to hear about NASA probes to Jupiter, to wonder what it would be like to have adventures in those places. They were as hungry as I was.

This hunger is what makes us human beings, different from dogs or cats who have no care for the Moon. To deny this to any person for any reason is to deny them their humanity.

God tells us to help the poor. But the goal of that help is not to make the poor wealthy. It's to be sure that everyone has the chance to have their physical needs taken care of, long enough that they can spare the time to feed their minds and souls. We do not live by bread alone ... none of us, whether you live on Lake Huron or Lake Naivasha.

What is the hunger that we satisfy by looking at the Moon? Why do we bother to look? Something about it stimulates our curiosity. It satisfies our souls. It brings us joy.

2

Learning to See

Science is more than observing the universe; it's a conversation with everyone else who's ever observed the universe, where we can talk about what has been observed and wonder about what to look for next. We need a community of fellow seekers to have those conversations. The other people in the conversation can teach us how to see, and keep us honest in evaluating what we think we have found. That's what separates true science (and true religion) from navel-gazing or basement philosophy.

NOTICE SOMETHING IN my story of 'finding myself' in the Peace Corps. I would not have been able to orient myself if I hadn't known the constellations before I got there. Notice something in my story of sharing a telescope with folks up country in small villages; that would not have been possible if I didn't have a telescope to share (invented by others, made by others, and indeed purchased because my friend Dan helped me buy it), and if I didn't know where to point it or what to look for. Likewise, if I had not spent ten years working on NASA grants studying the moons of Saturn, I would not have had the stories to tell them about the Voyager space probe or what it might be like to walk on Titan.

It wasn't enough to simply say, 'Oh, wow, look at the Moon' ... though that is a necessary first step. In order to feel at home in Africa, I had to have a history of having first learned the stars in my own home, far away from Africa. I needed to learn from my father, from my teachers, from my friends. I had to have books that could connect me to the traditional knowledge of my ancestors, those who first traced and named the constellations. (Curiously, many of those constellation names are the same all over the world, in many different cultures, predating any written records.)

And consider that little telescope I had brought with me. It was great for looking at the Moon and planets, but I soon became frustrated because I didn't know where else I could point it. Before I left, my friend Dan who'd helped me buy it showed me how to set it up, and he pointed it at a few fascinating double stars and stellar clusters. Looking at them through this new gizmo, with him beside me, was a surprise and a delight. But when I finally got to upcountry Kenya, all by myself and with a thousand different stars overhead, I couldn't remember which of them were the fun ones to look at. I needed a book to tell me where to point my telescope, the way that H. A. Rey had taught me the shapes and names of the constellations. (Eventually, Dan and I wrote that book.)

And where had Dan learned that stuff? To be able to know the stars, the constellations the double stars and nebulae, he had already entered into a community of people who had preserved that knowledge in magazines and books, housed in public libraries, where he could find it. That same community had invited me into the deeper study of astronomy in graduate school, which is where I learned how to interpret what those images mean, and what the community had come up with so far to explain them, and how we can go about learning even more, together as a community.

When I was assigned to be a lecturer in the physics department of the University of Nairobi, I became a link in that chain of study. It was my job to pass on some of that knowledge to a new generation of graduate students.

They may have been raised on a different continent from me, in a different culture from mine, but now they shared with me a common heritage of western physics. Our textbook for classical electrodynamics, for example, was an edition printed at low cost in India but otherwise identical to the one I had used at the University of Arizona. These students in turn would provide the next link; many of them had posts waiting for them at the Kenya Science Teachers College, to teach the teachers of the generations of Africans yet to come.

The sense of what it meant to be part of the community was, in an odd way, made starkly clear to me while I was in Kenya. One of the tasks of my job at the University was dealing with the sort of strange mail that every university physics department receives on a regular basis. I recall one particular letter that described in great detail some novel theory of space and time and then ended in a classic manner: 'What remains is filling in the details ... the chapter of further investigation into the underlying principles of nature is closed. And certain well cherished theories and principles will have to be abandoned.'

Every professional scientist gets letters like these all the time, from 'science enthusiasts' with new and unprecedented explanations that purport to solve all the mysteries of the universe. (Today as the director of the Vatican Observatory I am a special target; the letters I get now exhibit a creative blend of bizarre physics with weird spirituality.)

Back before the internet, such letters were often hand-written, filling every possible square inch of onion-skin paper. Nowadays they come in the email with oddly capitalized words and links to obscure web sites or lengthy YouTube videos. Alas, in the words of the famous theoretical physicist Wolfgang Pauli, the writers are not only not right; they are not even wrong.

At first it's tempting to laugh at the naïveté of the authors. But as I have grown older, such messages now fill me with a deep sadness.

I know why people write such letters. I know

why they feel this need to reach out to the rest of the world, and feel affirmed in their desire to figure out the universe. It's the same urge that made me want to do more than just read science fiction at MIT, and instead actually do the science itself. It's that same urge that makes us want to look at the Moon. It is what makes us human. There's nothing wrong, and everything right, with following that urge.

But the way they are trying to do so is doomed to failure. Without being part of the scientific conversation, from the inside, they won't advance the science even if they're right; no one will listen to them. And they won't get the feedback from their peers that helps to scratch the itch that got them to write us in the first place.

The sadness comes not just from feeling sorry for people who have heard a few bits of technical jargon and think they can show up us experts. (Us experts are plenty adept at showing up each other, thank you.) It's not even just a sorrow at the fruitless effort of clever minds who've not had the opportunity I had been given to spend the years it takes to learn the language of science and get invited to join into the conversation.

The sadness also comes because these good people are victims of some of the worst lies of our culture: that the true heroes of science are lone geniuses ... or that the goal of science is to be recognized with prizes and featured spots in cable television documentaries. Or worse, that the goal of science is to find answers.

They want to think of themselves as lone geniuses. But there are no lone geniuses. As children we've grown up on the stories of Thomas Edison and Alexander Graham Bell. But we don't hear nearly enough about the hundreds of technicians, the 'muckers' as they were called, whom Edison employed at Menlo Park. And what about the lawyers and businessmen who figured out how to build and maintain and pay for a network of wires and countless switchboard operators? Without them, Bell's invention would have been just a local curiosity.

Albert Einstein was certainly the genius behind Relativity. But he did not work in a vacuum. Hendrik Lorentz derived the equations for the contraction of space and time that Einstein's theory explained, and Hermann Minkowski (who taught Einstein) worked out the mathematical formalism that now lets scientists actually use Einstein's ideas today. Meanwhile, a number of astronomers starting with Arthur Eddington tested that theory through painstaking observations; without them, who would have taken it seriously?

We all know how Bill Gates provided the original operating system software for personal computers, and how Steve Jobs had the inspiration of making those computers friendly for the rest of us to use. But it was the burgeoning infrastructure of computer hobbyists in Cambridge and California who provided the ecology (and friends like Steve Wozniak) where Gates and Jobs could grow and flourish.

Now consider the temptation found in

many ages, but especially prevalent today, to find God without religion. As John Prine sang in his 1971 song *Spanish Pipedream*, it's the urge to 'try and find Jesus on your own'. One can argue just how satirical he was being at the time (read the rest of his lyrics!) but the phrase certainly resonates with an attitude common in our culture that distrusts relying on authority. Indeed, 'Question Authority!' was a popular slogan of my youth. ('Says who?' I always wondered.) The contemporary version is to be 'spiritual but not religious'.

But how are you going to even know that there is a Jesus to find, or a spirituality to seek, if you don't hear about Him from preachers or books (or at least snarky songs)?

A spirituality invented in your basement is likely to be as fruitful as a scientific treatise hand-written on onionskin paper. Without knowing the history of what has gone before, you wind up at best re-inventing the wheel. And you are stuck in your basement, you can't get out and join the conversation much less contribute to it.

I think back to those summers on Lake Huron. As the sun set, the grownups would bring out a case of beer and sit around a fire, talking about everything under the stars. We kids would hide in the shadows, hoping that no one would notice us and send us off to bed. Most of what they were talking about went over our heads, though I still remember phrases that puzzled or amused my eight-year-old self. ('The Nixon-Kennedy election could be a landslide either way, because it's so close!') We had no hope of joining into that conversation. But we loved being around it, listening in.

The goal of a conversation is not to come up with a final answer to whatever's being discussed ... just as the goal of science is not to arrive at a truth that will fit neatly into a list of solved problems at the back of a textbook. A good conversationalist hears what the others are saying and then adds a thought that makes the topic richer. A successful contribution makes us think about something more deeply, makes us see things in a new perspective; or maybe it just provides a good laugh. A good conversation is a source of joy. And a good conversation never ends.

We have all experienced joining a group of friends in the middle of their conversation. Only if you're rude will you try to hijack the flow with your own pet topic. Instead, if you are polite and you love your friends, you first listen to them. You have to know what they're talking about, and what's already been said, before you can contribute anything meaningful yourself.

In the world of science, that's called going to graduate school. And, yes, for social and economic reasons too many people have little or no chance to attend and flourish in a university at that level. That was another reason for me teaching physics at the University of Nairobi. (Are we making the same mistake in our religion?)

The next best thing to attending a university is to teach yourself by reading a lot of good books on the topic. Those books can report some of what the conversation has been about up to now. At the very least, they're a way that their authors can talk to you; without those books, you wind up just talking to yourself. But nowadays, anyone can publish anything and sell it over the internet for 99 cents. How do you know what's worth reading? How do you know which books have become a fruitful part of the conversation? How do you know which books are being answered by other books, and how to follow the subtle subtext of the conversation?

The sign of an autodidact, a self-educated person, is not that they are stupid or ignorant; quite the contrary. But they tend to see a field, the conversation, in the light of the first book on the topic that they happened upon. They might be lucky in that choice; it might be a book that indeed has shaped the conversation. But given the sheer number of books out there nowadays, the odds are against you.

And what motivates anyone to write those books in the first place? It's the same urge that moves the crazy letter writers to tell me about their latest discovery, that made me bring a telescope and slides to small villages in rural Kenya, to listen to songs about preachers telling me to find Jesus even if I won't listen to the preachers themselves. It's the desire to connect with another person. And that is but another way to connect with the universe.

And finally, there's another reason why we need a community to do science or religion. It's one that people don't always like to talk about. But the truth is, there are times — most of the time, to be honest — when the day-to-day life of a scientist can be tedious. You spend all day staring at a computer screen looking for progress that is so uncertain, or all night at the telescope taking one exposure after another looking for changes that may be significant over the span of a year but not over the span of a night. Burnout happens. It can be dramatic ('I'll join the Peace Corps!'), but actually much shallower dips in enthusiasm can be much more common, and much more destructive in the long run.

Every love relationship has its down

periods. That includes love of the sky, love of knowledge and study, love of doing science... even love of God, when you feel nothing but an aching emptiness while you try to be in God's presence. Without the strength of a community and a tradition to keep you committed, at times like that it is tempting to sigh sadly and give up; the feeling's gone and you just can't get it back.

But a commitment to a community just might be enough to carry you along through your dark night of the soul until you reach the next dawn. It is so often the case that what follows when you stick it out is even deeper and richer than you had ever experienced or imagined you could experience, before. And even if you never emerge from the darkness yourself, your support of the community can lay the groundwork for someone else's moment of enlightenment.

A strong tradition and a supportive community can let you not only endure and overcome, but even to find glory in the trial. The greater the doubts, the stronger the faith.

What is faith but the commitment to keep going even in the face of doubts, of ennui, of every excuse and reason to give up?

The issue is made all the harder by the fact that, at times, you really need to admit you were mistaken. Not every scientific hunch turns out to be fruitful. Not every love affair is meant to last forever. (Indeed, the hotter the fever the faster the flameout.) Not everything you think is a religious belief is correct.

So how do you tell the difference between something worth fighting through, and something that's nature's way of telling you to run away? Again, it is community. It's a set of friends you can trust to be with you when you're down, and to tell you the truth when you don't necessarily want to hear it. Even better, it's a time-tested system of discernment that can be with you when you make the decisions, large and small, of should I stay or should I go.

You need other people to help you see what can be very hard to see for yourself.

3

Learning to Imagine

God's presence in the universe is like the presence of water to a fish. If we find God equally, everywhere we look, how do we ever notice Him? How do we choose where to concentrate our gaze? We can get a clue of how to do this from how we do science: the tool we use is our human imagination.

SCIENCE IS MORE than observing the universe. It's learning how to concentrate on one aspect while setting aside, at least momentarily, all the other interesting aspects that can distract us from coming to a deeper knowledge of the Universe.

To give a simple example, if you look at Mars in a telescope using a red filter, all the red parts of the Martian surface turn dark while the not-red parts stay bright. The contrast brings out the dark regions (covered in red dust) versus the bright regions (which are just bare rock). A more sophisticated system puts a series of filters into a wheel; turn the wheel, step by step, and let the light from the telescope pass through each filter in turn. This gives you more detail about the surface features' colors and by inference their chemical composition.

That's how we collect scientific data,

dissecting whatever we're studying (the light from a planet, the body of a frog) to examine it piece by piece. But then we must go further. Science doesn't stop once you have a pile of data. You have to think about what you saw, try to see how the different pieces fit together, try to make sense of it all. And, ultimately, from what you have discovered, you hope to understand more deeply what was there all along but never noticed before, and what is next in line to be studied.

That understanding and that expectation is an act of the imagination. You can think you understand something if you can imagine what must be going on. You can test your understanding by looking for what you imagine you will see.

Unfortunately, what we see depends to an embarrassing degree on what we expect to see. Imagination is a filter that both makes things clear, and blocks out what might turn out to be important.

If you already know God is present in the universe, then you can see God everywhere;

but if you don't expect to find God, then God becomes invisible. Neither seeing God nor failing to see God proves anything about God's actual presence, only about what you expected to see in the first place. But that's only to be expected; God cannot be 'proved', neither by faith nor by science, God must be assumed (or denied) axiomatically, as an act of faith, and then we can build the rest of our logical understanding of the universe upon that axiom. That's how we make sense of what we see.

There's a tremendous danger here, of course. We can limit ourselves to finding only the answers we want to find by carefully choosing what axioms we decide to believe in. As Rabbi Jonathan Sacks noted in his book *The Great Partnership*, 'Freud said that religious faith was the comforting illusion that there is a father figure. A religious believer might say that atheism is the comforting illusion that there is no father figure, so that we can do what we like and can get away with it: an adolescent's dream.' How do we know that our axioms, our core beliefs, either way are not just wish fulfillment? Paul Simon, in his song *The Boxer*, puts it more simply: 'A man hears what he wants to hear and disregards the rest.' Indeed this insight can be found in scripture; Paul's second letter to Timothy warns about those who 'have an itch to hear what they want to hear'.

There's a famous video that shows two teams of players passing basketballs, dressed in black and white; and you're asked to count the number of passes that the team in white makes. In the middle of the video, a man in a gorilla suit walks through the players. More often than not, people busy counting basketball passes don't even see the gorilla. If our expectations of what we're looking for are too limited, we may wind up missing the gorilla in the room.

But it's even more than that. Seeing what you expect to see is not just a statement of what can go wrong if you're not open to seeing new things. To an important extent, having to make that kind of selection is inevitable and unavoidable. The philosophers of science (you can find writers as diverse as Pierre Duhem and Paul Feyerabend making this point) say that every observation is 'theory-laden'. We design an experiment only if we have an idea ahead of time about what the results should look like; otherwise, how can we find what we're looking for (or recognize its absence) in those results? And that's true about everything we do in real life. Without a set of previous experiences, and the generalizations we've made for ourselves out of them, we're as helpless as a newborn baby or a fish out of water when it comes to coping with reality. That's why a new place, or a new day, can make us feel disoriented and homesick until we can fit our new experiences into a familiar pattern of how we live.

But there's also a positive side to this. In science, as our theories develop we can go back to old data and mine out of it nuggets of information that we wouldn't have known to look for before. The classic example is gathering ancient Chinese descriptions of 'guest stars', which we now recognize as supernovas, and using them to calibrate the size of the universe according to the Big Bang. More generally, as we grow older and wiser we open ourselves to that special frisson when we suddenly understand something we'd seen a million times before, but now in a totally new way. It's an experience that leads you to say, 'Oh! That's what they were talking about!'

You may recognize it as one of the pleasures of a good mystery novel, when the detective suddenly ties together the clues with a new point of view and reveals all. It's no accident that we experience this sort of insight in the works of the imagination, like a mystery or a romance. Our imagination is what guides us to see what we expect, but it also guides us to see what we only previously may have imagined. It is what makes it possible for us to operate in this complicated universe and avoid information overload. Imagination is not truth; but it is what we use to integrate the truth. And it is what we use to situate the joy that might lead us to truth.

There is an intimate connection between

science, faith, and storytelling. Consider how a detective in a murder mystery imagines for each suspect how the crime might have been done, and then searches for clues to support or disprove that imagined story. Creating a story in our imagination is a key to how we do science. And it is key to the spirituality that I have been trained in as a Jesuit brother, most notably in the famous Spiritual Exercises of St Ignatius.

Here's a typical example of a spiritual exercise that a retreatant might be asked to undertake:

> *First Prelude ... how Our Lady went forth from Nazareth, about nine months with child ... see with the sight of the imagination the road from Nazareth to Bethlehem; considering the length and the breadth, and whether such road is level or through valleys or over hills; likewise looking at the place or cave of the Nativity, how large, how small, how low, how high, and how it was prepared ... see the persons; Our Lady and Joseph ...*

look, mark and contemplate what they are saying, and, reflecting on myself, to draw some profit ...

'See with the sight of the imagination.' By imagining the scene, the story of the nativity becomes more than a story, more than a theological conundrum, more than a greeting card. It becomes something that we can recognize as an experience real people actually lived through, and with our imagination we can taste what it must have been like if we were to live through it as well. We smell the air; taste the brackish water that relieves the thirst of a scorching sun; enjoy taking a load off our aching feet at the end of the long day's hike. And we can suddenly identify with the worry that Joseph and Mary must have had about this baby to come, whose presence makes no sense and yet makes all the world make sense.

It does something else in the process. By inserting ourselves into our imagined story of Bethlehem, two thousand years ago, we remove ourselves for the moment from today's quotidian aches and worries. Or, better, it transforms our actual sore feet of today to the sore feet on the road to Bethlehem. In this way we can orient where we are at this moment, with a moment when God was most manifestly incarnate in the world.

'And reflecting on myself, to draw some profit.' The point of the imaginative exercise isn't simply to be some voyeur into another person's life, even the life of a saint. It is to draw a lesson, to learn, to be changed ourselves as a result. To know something afterwards that we now realize we didn't know when we began the exercise. What we wind up doing in this imagining is creating a personal story in our mind to fit the setting described in the Gospel.

It's no accident that the Gospels, the heart of our Christian scripture, are stories and not theological discourses. Jesus teaches in parables. We can hear a story, evaluate it against our own human experience of life, question it, and by instinct draw a lesson from it. (Sometimes not the lessons intended, of course – like the guy who heard the story of the

Prodigal Son and asked, 'after the son finally goes back to his father, who's taking care of the pigs?') And you remember stories ... which is more than you can say about most of the letters of St Paul you hear on a Sunday.

Even beyond the parables, however, the Gospels themselves are stories. We do not just hear what Jesus said, we hear a story about where he was and to whom he was speaking. This makes the message more memorable, of course; it also puts the story into a context so that we can understand it better. It would be one thing to have a mere compilation of the sayings of Jesus (as indeed some scholars think might have existed before the Gospels as we know them were written). But a phrase like 'render to Caesar what is Caesar's but to God what is God's' is far more powerful, and means so much more, when it is placed in the setting of enemies trying to trap Jesus.

Science fiction stories were what first made planets feel like real places to me; the stories I read as a teenager inspired me to learn to do the science I do as an adult. But in fact, every scientific paper is itself a story. A technical paper is an artificial retelling of something that really happened. It even follows the classical form of a story: exposition, rising action, climax, falling action, denouement. You describe the problem. You describe why it's a problem – and why you needed that clever or difficult or special thing you did, to make it all work. You describe your brilliant contribution. You describe what came of it. And then you sit back, see how it changes all our ideas about the universe, and why you'll be asking for another grant next year to keep up the good work.

Just as prayer is a spiritual exercise, research is the exercise of someone who wants to be a scientist. It's pretty common nowadays for undergraduates in the sciences to get involved with research projects, but back when I was a student at MIT it was a new and exciting idea. My first project was notable only for the equipment I wound up breaking. (Remember those filter wheels I talked about? I bounced one down a set of metal stairs). So when I got my courage up enough to try again I chose a more theoretical topic.

My advisor had the idea that the moons of Jupiter and Saturn, made of a mixture of rock and ice, might actually be molten inside due to the little bit of heat emitted from the rocky bits by the traces of radioactive elements that all rocks contain. The trick was to flesh out this idea, calculate how much heat would actually be generated, how much it would build up, and where it would go inside a thousand-mile-wide iceball over the age of the solar system — some four billion years plus change. I started working on this during my junior year, writing my computer code during the summer of 1973 while watching the Watergate hearings on television.

But how do you 'write computer code' to model the interior of an icy moon? No one had ever done it before, including my professor. I had to invent it as I went along. Indeed, that was so long ago that even the basic principles of good computer programming hadn't been worked out yet; what I produced was in fact a tangled mess of poorly documented Fortran spaghetti, full of do-loops and go-to statements.

But before I could write a line of code, I had to do something even more basic. I had to figure out just what it was I was trying to model. In other words, before I could write a line of code to model a moon's evolution, I had to imagine it in my mind's eye.

I remember where I was when I first started daydreaming about the interiors of icy moons: staying with my cousins at their home outside Schenectady, New York, during the spring of 1973 ... Easter break, perhaps? I recall lying on the bed in their guest room, staring at the ceiling, and picturing a little movie of what would happen inside a melting moon.

The heat comes from radioactive elements; but the abundance of radioactive elements decreases as time goes on — after a half-life, half of them will have decayed away, so then the amount of heat you get will have dropped by a half. Note to self: include lines of code with the equation that keeps track of the exponential drop in the amount of heat produced over time. Oh, and find out the most important radioactive elements (it turns out those are Potassium 40, Uranium 235 and 238, Thorium 232) and how fast they decay (look up the half-lives in the library) and how much heat a gram of each would give off (a table from another book), and how much you'd expect to find of each of these elements in the rocky stuff. I guess the composition of the rocky stuff should probably not be all that different from the meteorites we have in our collections today; find a good book about meteorites that'll have that information. I see a lot of library work in my immediate future.

The heat goes into the surrounding rock and ice, heating it up. Note to self: how much heat does it take to change the temperature of the rock and ice mixture by one degree? The heat also flows out toward the surface of the moon, which is kept at the ambient cold temperature of space. How cold? That depends on how far the moon is from the Sun. Note to self: should I calculate that temperature? Or just look up what everyone uses for the temperatures of the cloud tops of Jupiter and Saturn?

When the temperature at any given point inside the moon reaches the melting point of ice, then the temperature stops rising while heat goes into turning the ice into water ... I remember in high school chemistry watching mothballs over a burner keep a constant temperature while they melted. Time for an 'if/then' statement, and define another variable to keep track of the latent heat. Oh, and the melting point at any given spot inside the moon will depend on the pressure that the ice is feeling there. Calculate those pressures. Another set of computer code to write.

But wait; once the ice starts to melt, the rocks will fall through the water. They give up some potential energy doing that. That also gets turned into heat. But wait; if the rocks fall down, then some of the water has to go upwards to make room for the rocks, and that'll take energy away from the heat. But as the water moves upwards, that will carry heat with the molten water up to the regions where the water hasn't melted yet ...

In my mind's eye I pictured this big ball of dirty mush slowly melting, the warm water rising towards the surface and the hot rocky bits sliding downwards through the slush. How long would it take? How fast would the slush move? For my purposes, did that matter?

I won't go further into the details of what I got right and wrong. The resulting thesis was good enough for a master's degree, which is all that has endured. After half a century of spacecraft missions to visit those moons, my daydreams have been replaced with real data and images. But my imagination — and of course the imagination of my thesis advisor — played an essential role in those missions. Because we had imagined what the moons might look like, and worked out with mathematics the implications of one possible history over another, we were able to look at the spacecraft images and pick out the signs that would be tell-tale indicators of what had happened inside those moons. Without imagination we wouldn't have been able to know what to look for or appreciate what it was we were seeing.

And yet, I *was* wrong. Turns out, I had guessed the wrong values for many of the numbers I inserted into the equations. I had failed to imagine all the other things that could heat up or cool down a moon (the motion of the slush was important after all). I had imagined a much too simple starting point, a much too simple mix of materials, a much too simple description for how the heat would flow within them and about them.

And that's how progress is made: not just by admitting we were wrong (we're always wrong!) but outlining exactly where we went wrong. The first time your imagination comes up with a picture that seems to fit all the pieces together and shows you new things to look for, you get a little jolt of joy. But the first time you realize where that theory goes wrong, you also get a jolt of joy, because you're learning something new, something you'd

missed before, something that you can't wait
to tell your colleagues about.

Imagination plays one final role in our
conversations, both of science and of religion.
Once we've learned something, we have to
return to the conversation and add our piece.
When we talk about the universe (or we talk
about God) we are trying to get across ideas
and insights of things beyond our power to
comprehend, much less describe: unfamiliar,
esoteric insights. The language we must use
is, inevitably, that of poetry: the interior of
this moon is *like* the output of this computer
model ...

And poetry draws heavily on the
imagination. We use words that are familiar
and comfortable but which evoke deeper
meanings, associated with a particular place
or time. Think of song lyrics that we connect
with important years in our lives, like when
we were in college or when we fell in love. You
may have noticed the allusions to song lyrics
I've used throughout this piece. In a couple of
cases I've called out the song and the artist;

more often, however, I've slipped in phrases or patterns of words from popular songs in a way that you might not even have noticed. (A lot of them come from artists of the 1960s and 1970s; to spot them, it helps if you're an aging baby boomer like me.) It's deliberate. It gives a sense of familiarity to a topic that might feel intimidating at first. And if I have done it right, it also evokes an emotional connection that the mere words themselves, phrased differently, would have lacked.

Conclusion: Finding God in the Universe

My first act as an astronomer is to go outside at night and bend my head upwards. I must look beyond the mundane world of 'what's for lunch' to see the Moon and the stars and the planets. But then I have to engage what I see with my reason. To do that I need an education; that is where I discover the conversations of fellow astronomers. They create the playing field where what I have seen can fit into what the human race has seen so far, and let me make a small but real contribution to what we'll look for next. And finally, I have to open up my imagination to make what goes on in the universe also something that goes joyfully into my soul. This joy informs me, and inspires me to keep looking.

I encounter God with the same tools that I use to encounter the Universe: my senses, my reason, and my imagination. That is to say,

I use everything that makes me human: my liberty, my memory, my understanding, and my entire will, all that I have and possess ... which God has given to me, and thus I can offer it to God to dispose of according to His will. Science is not only an act of prayer in the generic sense of an encounter with the Creator; it is also the specific prayer of the *Suscipe* of St Ignatius.

Spending my childhood summers on the shores of Lake Huron, that wild and cold fresh water sea, I could devote hours to just looking at the water and the waves. But more often, that wasn't enough. I wanted to run along the beach, jump full force into the waves, sail across the water to the distant Canadian shore. (I remember once when my father and I did just that ... sixty-five kilometers from Port Sanilac to Grand Bend, in a 25-foot Folkboat sloop. All day to get there. That's half a century ago, now. The joy of first touching a distant shore that we'd sailed to, by ourselves, I'll never forget.)

Leaping headlong into the universe is what

we humans do: as scientists, as artists, as people of prayer. It is accepting and returning the loving embrace of creation and its Creator. That is my theology.

Gallery

In my early 30s, I abandoned science to join the US Peace Corps; here I am by the side of the road to Eldoret, Kenya, in 1984, much slimmer and not as grey as I am today. I had thought studying astronomy was useless in a world of hunger and need. But the Kenyans knew better. They were hungry to learn about astronomy; they did not live by bread alone.

In the mid-1930s, the Vatican installed two state-of-the-art Zeiss telescopes on the roof of the Pope's summer palace in Castel Gandolfo. This is one is an unusual design called a 'Double Astrograph', where two telescopes share one mounting. It was used by a team of astronomer-priests and brothers at the Vatican Observatory to photograph stars and their spectra until the 1980s, when light pollution from Rome had turned the night sky milky white.

Did you ever notice how the crescent Moon is always seen near the horizon at dusk or dawn? The lit side of the Moon faces towards the Sun. This photo, from Tucson, Arizona, shows the Moon curved like the letter 'C'; the observant astronomer thus knows that the photo was taken early in the morning, just before dawn. On a line between the Moon and where the Sun is about to rise, you can also see another bright dot, the planet Venus. No fancy equipment was needed for this photo; I just used my cell phone camera during a morning walk.

Through even a small telescope, like Galileo had, one can see that the Moon is covered with round craters and the occasional flat dark region. The big fresh crater in this image is the crater Tycho, named after the astronomer whose cosmology was the best rival to Copernicus. Copernicus also has a crater. Both names were given to the craters by the Jesuit priest Fr Giovanni Battista Riccioli. This image was taken by a large refractor (40cm aperture) on the roof of the Papal Palace in Castel Gandolfo.

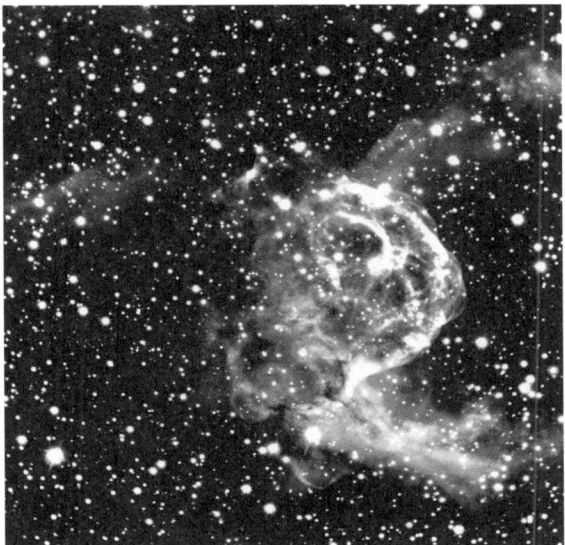

The sky is full of stars. But in addition, with a big mirror telescope like the Vatican's Advanced Technology Telescope outside of Tucson, Arizona, you can make out faint clouds of light called 'nebulae'. This object, numbered NGC 2359 in the New Galactic Catalog ('new' as of the late-nineteenth century!), has the nickname 'Thor's Helmet'. It is a cloud of gas and dust, the debris of an exploded star, 30 light years across and located 12,000 light years away from us, illuminated by a small but powerful nearby star.

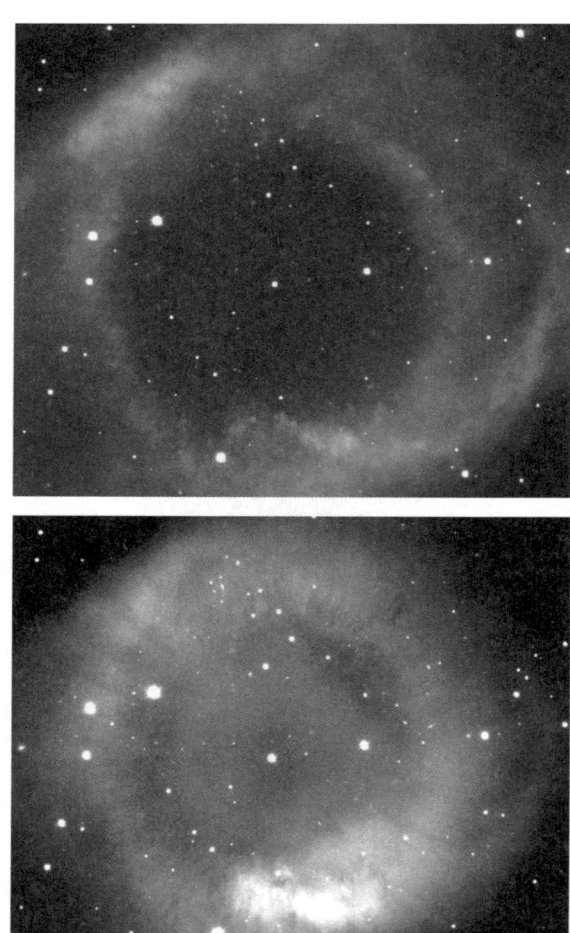

86

The Helix nebula is a bubble of gas and dust emitted from a dying star; it's located 660 light years away from Earth. We can tell what gases are present by their characteristic colours, and so we show here three different images taken through red (upper left), green (left), and blue (above) filters at the Vatican Advanced Technology Telescope outside of Tucson, Arizona. The light emphasised in the red filter image is emitted by hydrogen gas, while the bright parts seen only in the green filter image show the presence of oxygen.

MY THEOLOGY

ANN LOADES
THE SERENDIPITY OF LIFE'S ENCOUNTERS

'Discovering theology came about by sheer accident,' writes Ann Loades, one of the most distinguished theologians of our time – only the second person to be awarded a CBE for 'services to theology'.

The Serendipity of Life's Encounters charts the particular challenges facing a schoolgirl of the 1950s attracted to the possibility of going to university to read Theology, and her fascinating subsequent path to becoming the first woman to be given a personal Chair at the University of Durham.

Pertinent themes explored include women in theology, worship, engagement with actual living, biography and theology in various writers.

M Y T H E O L O G Y

The world's leading Christian thinkers explain some of the principal tenets of their theological beliefs.

Collect the full library.

September 2021

1. Robert Beckford
2. Ilia Delio
3. Malcolm Guite
4. Alister McGrath

November 2021

5. Guy Consolmagno
6. Ann Loades
7. Rachel Mann
8. Keith Ward

January 2022

9. Cynthia Bourgeault
10. Grace Ji-Sun Kim
11. John Swinton
12. Mpho Tutu van Furth

March 2022

13. Joan Chittister
14. Scot McKnight
15. Siku